THIS WALKER BOOK BELONGS TO:

This book was bought with
money gifted to the
nursery by the Deyell
family, in memory of their
late father, Bertie Deyell
of Semblister, Bixter.

There are more than 150 different
kinds of octopus, and the Giant
octopus is the biggest — the tentacles
of the largest one ever found
were an amazing 4.8 metres long!

Even though they are so huge,
Giant octopuses do not attack humans.
They live in coastal waters in the
north Pacific Ocean, and feed mainly
on crabs, clams and sea snails.

Female Giant octopuses only ever
lay eggs once in their lives.
They are thought to eat little or
nothing after mating, and once
their eggs have hatched,
female octopuses die.

For Mariana Shnaider
K.W.

For J.W. & A.W., with love
M.B.

Consultant: Martin Jenkins

First published 1998 by Walker Books Ltd
87 Vauxhall Walk, London SE11 5HJ

This edition published 2000

2 4 6 8 10 9 7 5 3 1

This book has been typeset in Calligraphic.

Printed in Hong Kong

British Library Cataloguing in Publication Data
A catalogue record for this book is
available from the British Library.

ISBN 0-7445-7290-8

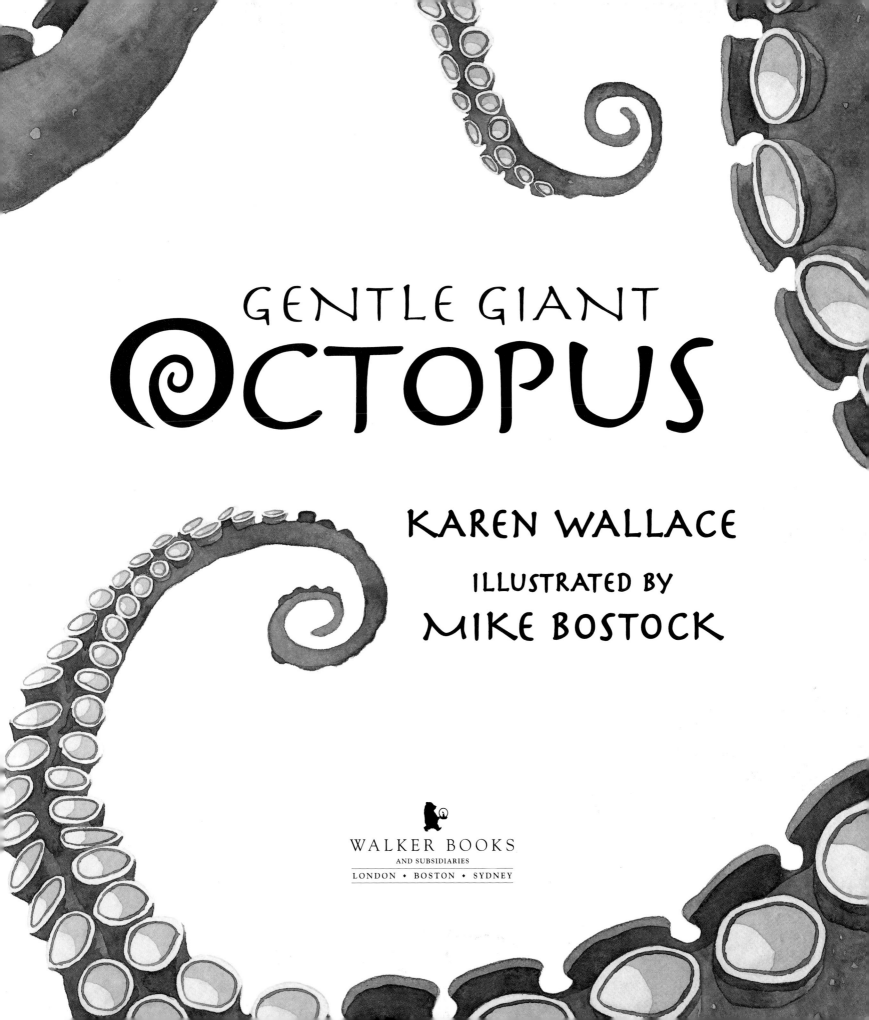

GENTLE GIANT
OCTOPUS

KAREN WALLACE

ILLUSTRATED BY
MIKE BOSTOCK

WALKER BOOKS
AND SUBSIDIARIES
LONDON • BOSTON • SYDNEY

A gentle Giant octopus
jets through the shadows.
She's huge like a spaceship.
Her eyes glow in the water.
Long tentacles fly like
ribbons behind her.
Silver-backed fish
scatter before her.

6

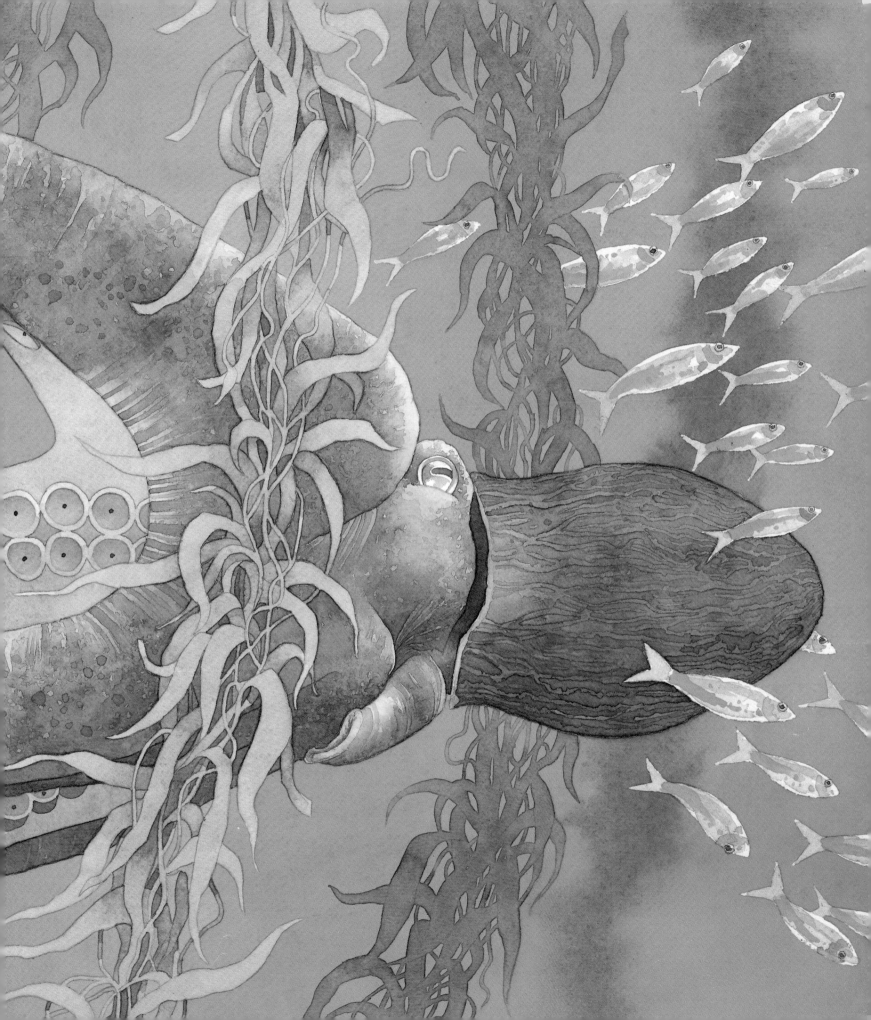

A wandering mother octopus
moves through the water.
Inside her body, she carries her eggs.
She looks for a den that is safe
and well hidden,
for a crack in a rock face or
a hole under a stone.

When octopuses need to move quickly,

they jet backwards by sucking in sea water

and pumping it out through a funnel-like siphon.

An octopus sinks
like a huge
rubber flower.

10

Sand muddies the water
as she lands on
the seabed.

Octopuses use their tentacles like fingers to sense things.

They use the suckers on their tentacles to grip things.

Octopus eyes turn
frontwards and backwards.
Her tentacles sense
a crab in the water.
A tentacle searches.
It stretches
and touches...

Unlucky
octopus!

14

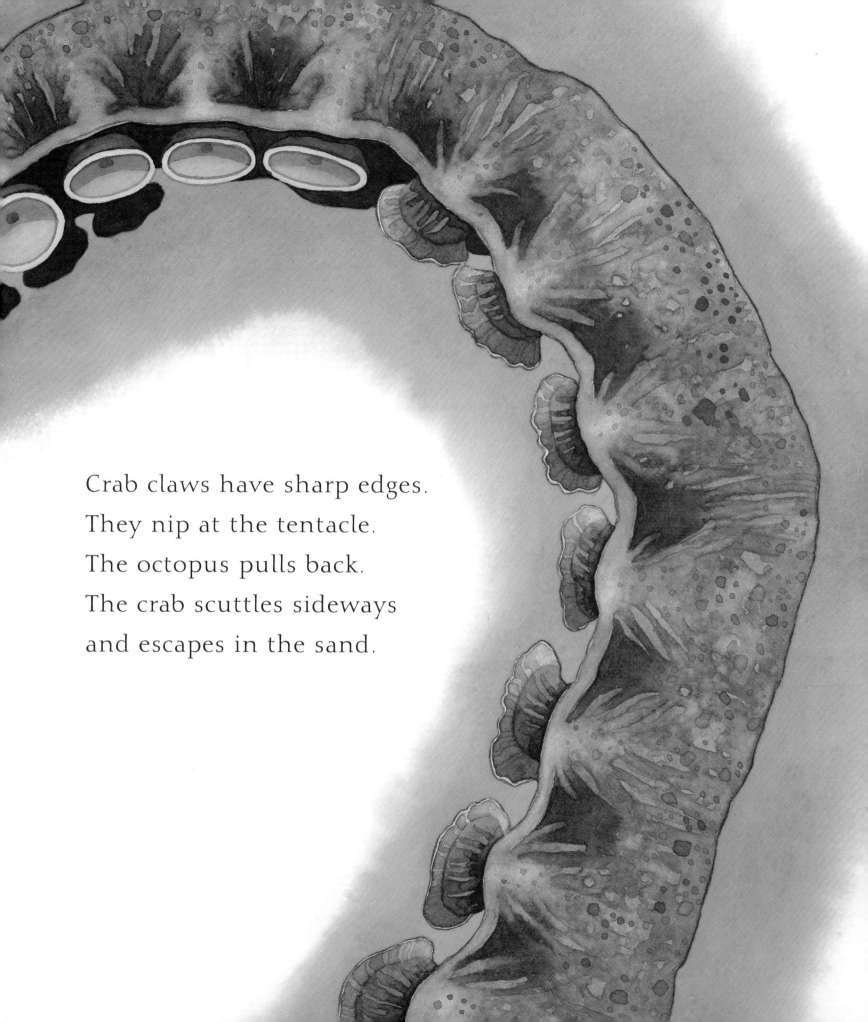

Crab claws have sharp edges.
They nip at the tentacle.
The octopus pulls back.
The crab scuttles sideways
and escapes in the sand.

A mother Giant octopus
slides over the seabed.
Her body stretches like toffee
over the stones.
Her skin ripples like seaweed.
She's black as the sea kelp.
The goggle-eyed octopus
feels her way forwards.

Usually the Giant octopus is reddish brown, but when it's hunting or hiding it can change to become very dark or very pale within seconds.

16

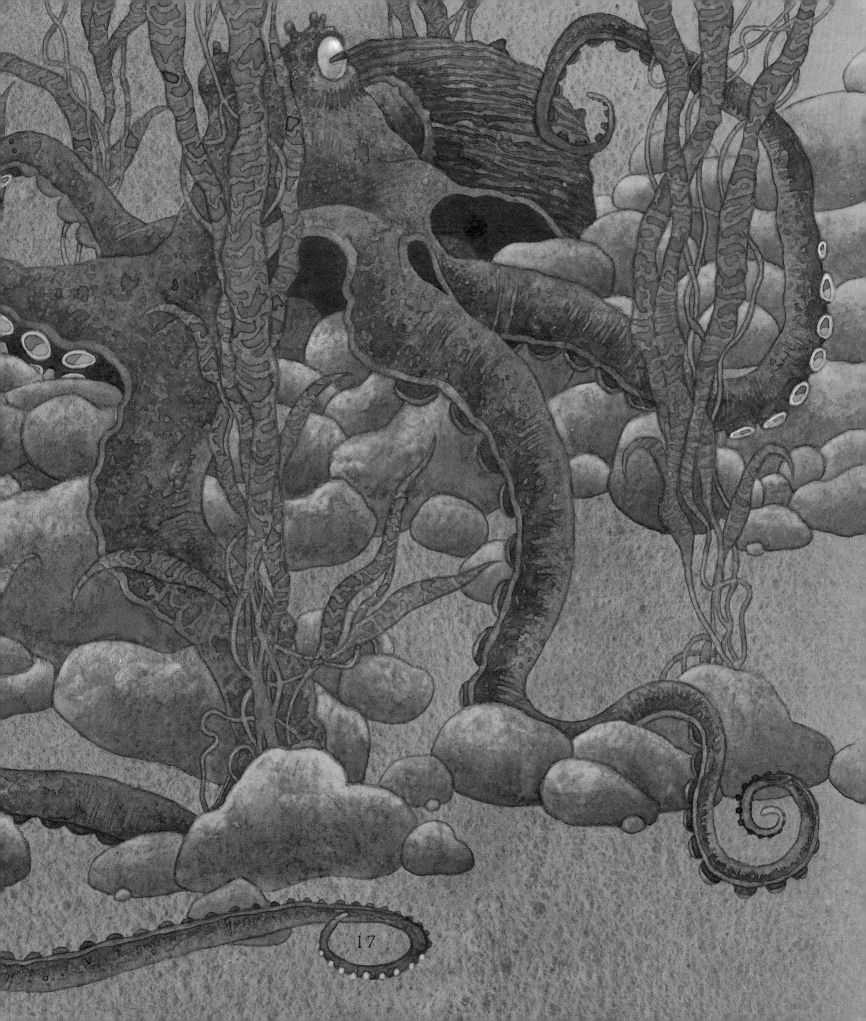

But under a boulder,
a Wolf-eel is waiting.
His mottled grey face darts
from the shadows.
His teeth strike
like daggers.
He rips off
a tentacle.

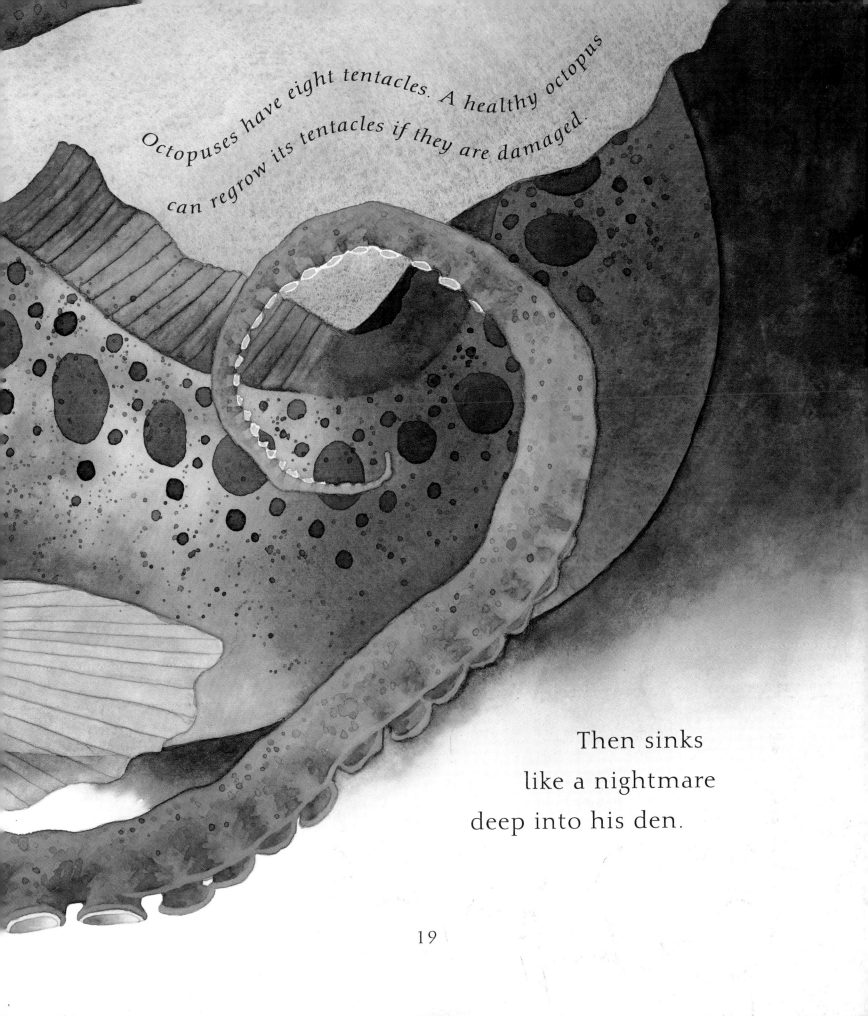

Octopuses have eight tentacles. A healthy octopus can regrow its tentacles if they are damaged.

Then sinks
like a nightmare
deep into his den.

If an octopus is attacked,
it will squirt out a cloud of inky liquid to hide its escape.

20

A frightened Giant octopus
squirts ink at the Wolf-eel.
She shoots back from the boulder,
back over the seabed.
She's pumping and sucking
the sea from her body.

21

A quivering Giant octopus
rests on a boulder.

Underneath is a cave
that is easily guarded.

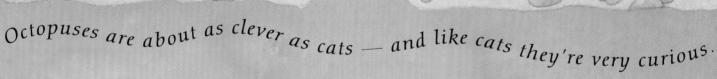

Octopuses are about as clever as cats — and like cats they're very curious.

She squeezes inside.
She drags pebbles around her.

Her search for a home
is over at last.

Octopuses don't have any bones, and they can squeeze through the tiniest of holes.

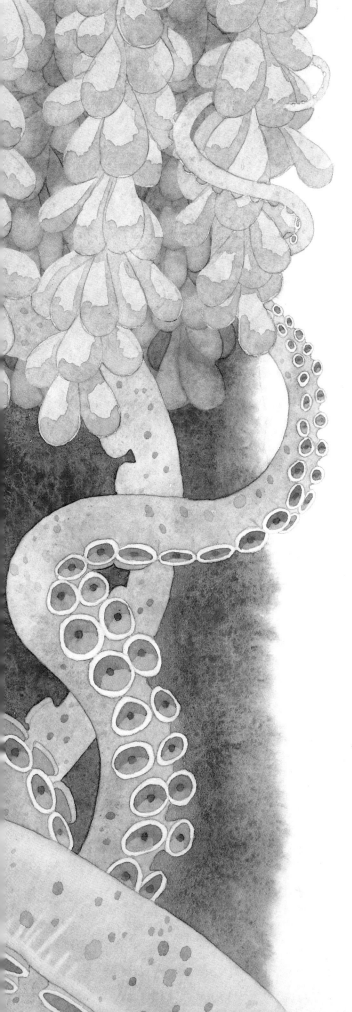

A mother Giant octopus lays
eggs in her cave den.
They hang from the roof
like grapes on a string.
She guards them from crabs
and nibbling fishes.
While her babies are growing,
she never eats and never rests.

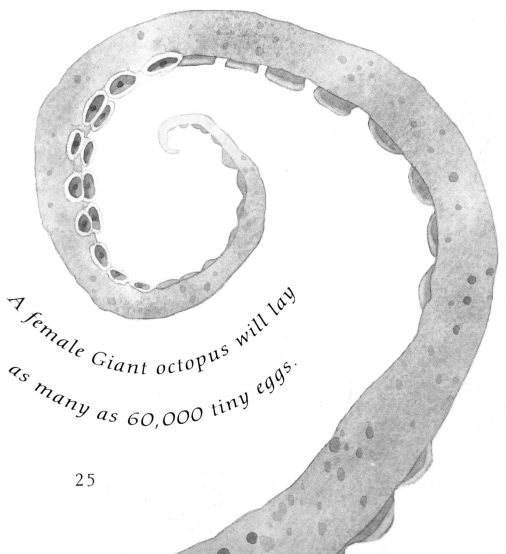

A female Giant octopus will lay
as many as 60,000 tiny eggs.

25

After five months her babies
swim from their egg sacs.
They squirm and they wiggle.
They jet through the shadows.
They're sucking and pumping
the sea from their bodies.

Lots of other animals like to eat baby octopuses, so only two or three out of every brood live to become adults.

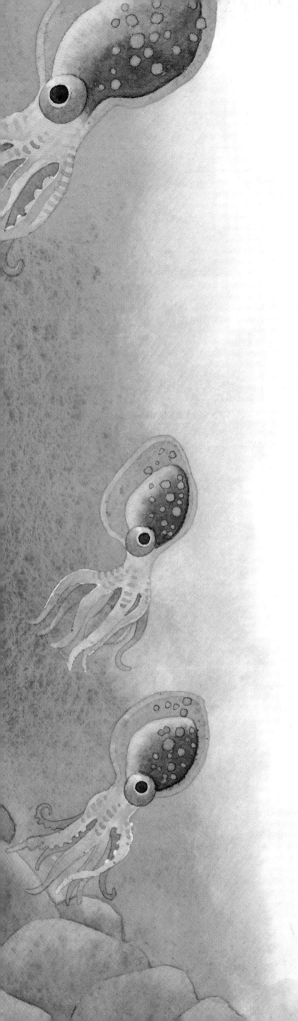

A mother Giant octopus
rests in her cave den.
She watches her babies
swim up through
the water.

A gentle Giant octopus
shrinks in the shadows.
Her life is over as their lives begin.

Index

Look up the pages to find out
about all these octopus things.
Don't forget to look at both kinds
of word — this kind
and *this kind*.

About the Author

Octopuses have a special place
in Karen Wallace's imagination — from
the storybook monsters of folklore, to the young
octopus she watched escape from a fish trap,
climb down a boat ladder, and sink back to the
safety of the sea. Karen's many picture books
about animals include *Bears in the Forest*, *Red Fox*,
My Hen Is Dancing, *Think of a Beaver*, and
Think of an Eel, which won the Kurt Maschler
and TES Junior Information Book Awards.

About the Illustrator

Mike Bostock became fascinated by octopuses
while illustrating this book — the delicate,
changing colour and texture of their skin,
the rubbery rippling way they move, their
transparent soap-bubble-like babies.
Mike's other picture books for Walker
include the award-winning *Think of an Eel*
by Karen Wallace, and *A Song of Colours*
by Judy Hindley.

More Walker non-fiction picture books for you to enjoy

ISBN 0-7445-3639-1 (pb)

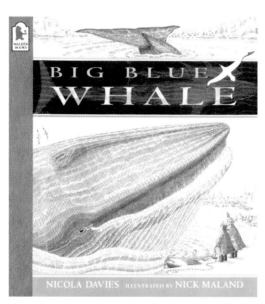

ISBN 0-7445-6300-3 (pb)

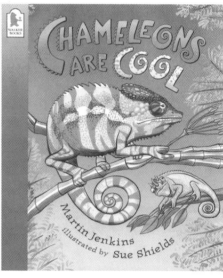

ISBN 0-7445-6333-X (pb)

ISBN 0-7445-4361-4 (pb)

ISBN 0-7445-3638-3 (pb)

ISBN 0-7445-4734-2 (pb)

FOR THE BEST CHILDREN'S BOOKS, LOOK FOR THE BEAR.